DOODLE diary

Art Journaling for Girls

DAWN DEVRIES SOKOL

GIBBS SMITH
TO ENRICH AND INSPIRE HUMANKIND

For my husband, TJ,
who always supports me
no matter what

and for my niece, Sienna,
who inspires me more
than she knows.
Keep journaling, girl!

First Edition
16 15 14   20 19 18 17

Text © 2010 Dawn DeVries Sokol
Illustrations © 2010 Dawn DeVries Sokol

Published by
Gibbs Smith
P.O. Box 667
Layton, Utah 84041

1.800.835.4993 orders
www.gibbs-smith.com
www.dblogala.com

Designed by Dawn DeVries Sokol
Manufactured in China in January 2014 by Toppan Printing Co.
Gibbs Smith books are printed on either recycled, 100% post-consumer waste,
FSC-certified papers or on paper produced from a 100% certified sustainable forest/
controlled wood source.

ISBN 13: 978-1-4236-0529-4
ISBN 10: 1-4236-0529-2

also work great for images of people and objects. Turn the magazine upside down while flipping through to see patterns and shapes you might not otherwise notice.

CUT AND PASTE

Try various ways of pasting and attaching items to pages, such as different tapes, staples, brads, stickers, labels, photo corners . . .

HANDWRITING

Writing along with doodling makes it even more of a diary! Mixing words with visuals is fun!

WORD ART

IF you don't like your own handwriting, there are some ready-doodled words at the back of this book. You can also cut out words and letters from used magazines and junk mail, or print out words from your computer.

rUBBEr STAMPS

Alphabet rubber stamps are a great way to "write" in your diary, too! Ink pads come in all colors now.

OUTLINING

Try outlining images you paste down. If you're working on a colored page, use a pen/marker/crayon that will match that color somewhat. This blends the image into the page. You can also use Wite-Out pens on dark backgrounds.

❀ TiPS

* If you make a mistake, just doodle or collage over it. Mistakes usually lead to better art.

* Tool Tips are included throughout as suggestions. Follow or ignore them — it's up to you!

* There are blank pages with colored backgrounds throughout the book. Use these to doodle whatever you would like.

* Let your mind wander as you doodle. You never know what great ideas will pop up.

Have FUn!

—I don't know

TOOLS to USE

COLORED PENCILS

of any kind will work.

WATERCOLOR PENCILS

These look like colored pencils except they can turn into watercolor on the page. Simply color on the page then use a wet paintbrush or wet your fingertip and smudge in. You can also dip the pencil tip in water and color that way.

NUMBER 2 PENCILS

are great, too!

BLACK PENS

There are all kinds: Micron, Prismacolor, and Pitt Pens. Play with whatever you can.

GEL PENS

Available in craft, art, and office supply stores, these pens leave great color on your pages. Use them to fill in doodles.

SOUFFLÉ PENS

These pens are like gel pens and are becoming more widely available in various stores. Pastel-colored, their ink puffs up a little on the page when dry. A great opaque soufflé pen shows up well when used on dark papers.

BIC OR SHARPIE PENS

These pens are good for doodling and come in a wide variety of colors, although they CAN bleed through to the other side of the paper.

* CRAYOLA PIP SQUEAKS

The Pip Squeaks work well — the colors are more like watercolors, not as bright as other pens, but shouldn't bleed through paper. They're widely available and inexpensive, too!

CRAYONS

Crayons are great, too, as a last touch — for drawing borders around images and adding color.

PORTFOLIO OIL PASTELS BY CRAYOLA

These work like watercolor pencils . . . use as a last touch: trying to draw over these with any pen will only stop up the pen. You can smear oil pastels into the paper with a fingertip and can also color in with a bit of water.

*Ways to attach ITEMS:

GLUE

* Paper Clips

* Glue sticks are less messy than regular glue

MOD PoDGE

* Use on corners of items or all around edges

+tape

* Any dry roller tape glue works

Tombo MONO

You Also Need

* Small scissors to make cutting out tiny items easy

* 1 or 2 cheap paintbrushes

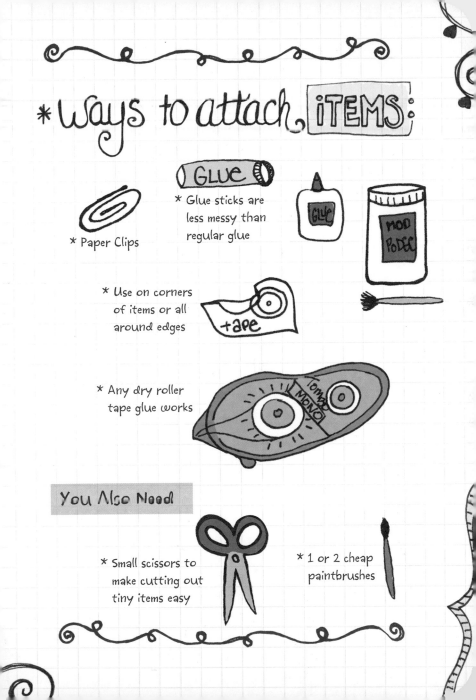

LiNE doodles

Sometimes, it's fun to doodle in a straight line up or across your page, adding on little bits as you go. Fill your page with lines of stars, vines with leaves, "stitched" lines, a heartbeat line, swirly lines, hearts . . .

DOODLES
of MY DAY

❀ What happened today?
→ Doodle and write about your day's events.

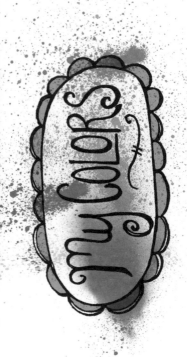

My Colors

Use these two pages to scribble your favorite colors, then doodle around them. Label the colors and use varying shades. Make it fun!

TOOL TIP:

* Use a combo of pens, markers, colored pencils, and crayons.

MeHNDi ARTWORK~

From India, Africa,
and the Middle East.
Lots of curly lines,
half circles, and dots.
Just keep adding on!
It's SO easy!

Cut out a photo of
a friend — paste onto the page
and start doodling in the
Mehndi style around it.

Try flowers, swirls, butterflies, and peace symbols — fun! Use bright rainbow-like colors.

HAPPY CHICK FLOWER

graffiti style

Art is inspiring, but when done with doodles and a journal, NOT on a wall! This doodling style can be girly with flowers, spirals, dots, and swirls.

TOOL TIP:
Try using a Wite-Out pen to doodle on the darker areas.

doodle
SPLOTCHES

Ink splatters make a great starting point for doodles. Use these pages to doodle around or from the ink spots. Go to it — fill the page!

My favorite **SONG**

Write down some of the words from your favorite song, doodle around them, then add colors it brings to mind. How does it make you feel?

SINGER

Find a photo/
paste it down.
➡Doodle.

STiCK iT!

Cover this page with stickers and doodle around them.

favorite actor ⭐

TOOL TIP:

To cut out people from photos, use small scissors to get into tiny crevices. The smaller point helps to cut in narrow areas.

favorite actress

i LiKe to EAT...

(List, doodle, collage the foods
you ♥, including dessert)

CHIN-
ESE

My Pet...

Include photos or draw your pet on these two pages. If you don't have a pet, doodle or collage your dream pet. Add its name, food bowl, collar, favorite sleeping spot, or other details.

QUOTED

Use these pages to doodle
favorite quotations, whether they
be from books, movies, songs,
or something a friend said.

TIP 8 Cut and paste words from magazines. Rubber stamps are cool, too!

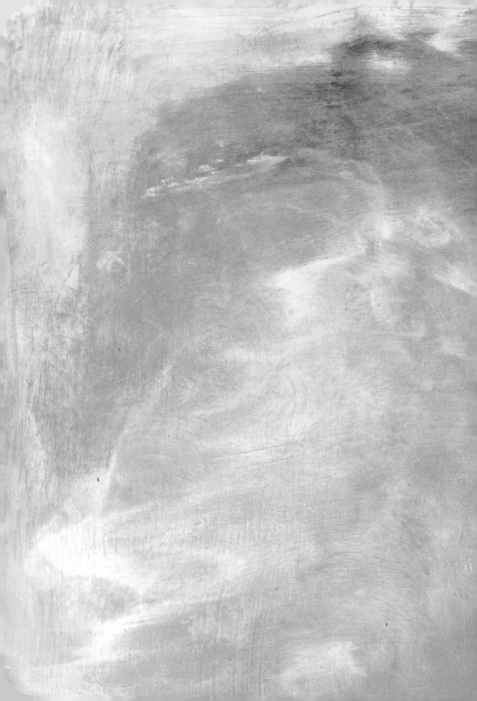

MY HOLIDAY

Doodle your favorite holiday, using colors, symbols, and shapes that reflect that holiday. Paste images, too!

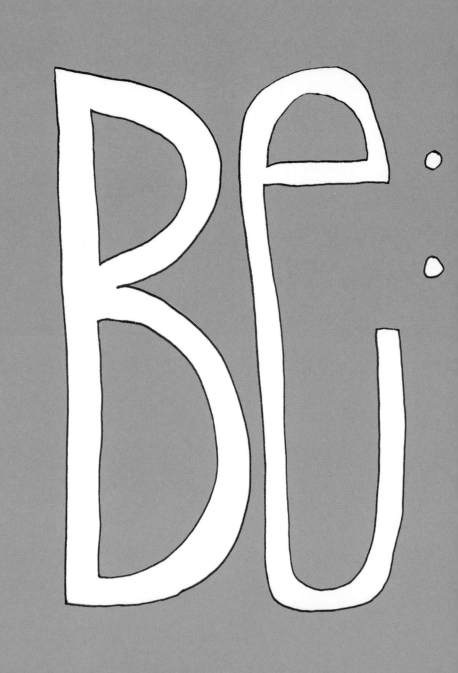

What do I want to be? Happy, adventurous, fun? Either write these words or find them in magazines and paste them onto the page. Doodle around them.

Also, doodle inside "Be" or color it in.

extreme SCHOOL Makeover

Got a photo of your school? Paste it onto the page and doodle over it to "remake" it.

BABY, i'M A ST★R!

If you were a star, which kind would you be and why? Rock star, reality star, social celebrity, best-selling author, fashion designer?

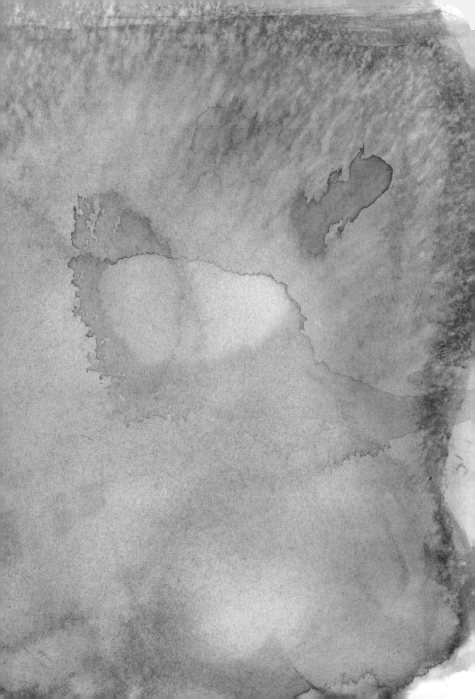

WHAT makes

me HAPPY?

tool TIP: Mix things up a bit and use a little watercolor pencil here and there. Color in with pencil, then wet your fingertip a little and rub the color into the page. Watercolor without the mess!

DOODLE MY WARDROBE

Paste down a photo of you (head and neck),
then doodle the rest of you with clothes
you want to have in your closet. You can
also use images from magazines.

LEFTY ~ RIGHTY

If you are right-handed, doodle on this page using only your left hand. If you are a lefty, doodle on this page using only your right hand.

GLAD to Have _____ IN MY LIFE Because...

Doodle, collage, and write about the people and things you are happy to have around.

toolTiP:

Use a Portfolio crayon to lightly outline the photos and pieces you paste down. Smear it into the paper with your fingertip.

PORTFOLIO

WORDS to USE:

WORDS NOT to use:

my MOVIE Reviews

Add your comments on movies you see . . .
Add ticket stubs, photos from ads, etc.

Least fave CLASS/subject

(My reviews of books)

What I've READ

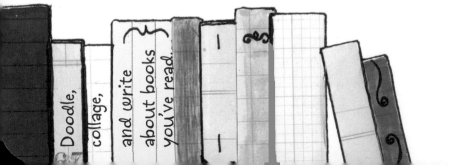

Doodle, collage, and write about books you've read.

My EMBARRASSING MOMENTS:

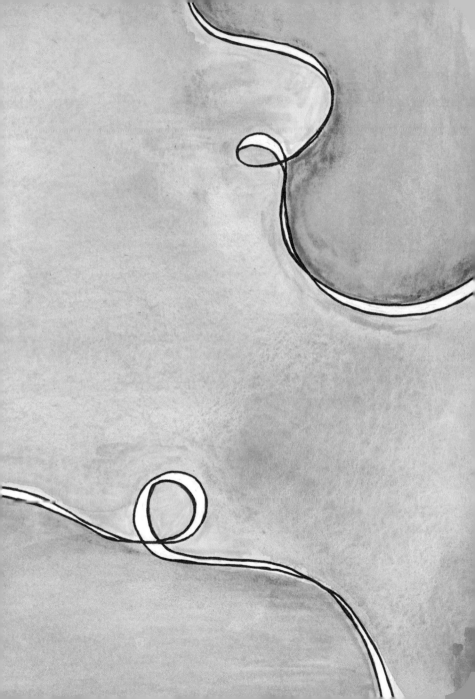

Watercolor

Doodle on this page using
only watercolor colored pencils.

To BE an ADULT
Because...

WHAT'S IN MY BAG / BACKPACK

MY HEROES

TIP: Paste photos or write the names of your heroes and doodle around them.

JUST GELLING!

Doodle on this page using only gel pens.

CLIP IT!

Cut out pictures of things you like from magazines, glue them down here, and doodle around them.

My favorite CLOTHING

Collage, write, and doodle!

MY FUTURE SELF

What do you want to be in life?
List careers you might want to
explore. Doodle and collage!

my favorite
JEWELRY

Find photos, collage, write, and doodle!

my INSPIRATIONS

Find + include colors, words, patterns, illustrations, labels, photos . . . What is so inspiring about these? These pages will help pump you up in your diary + other art when you feel stuck.

WHAT i FOUND TODAY:

Paste down that cool candy wrapper, earring, ribbon, straw wrapper, dollar bill, leaf, flower, business card, or sticker from where you ate lunch.

COMBINE COLLAGED WORDS and DOODLES

FIND random words in old magazines, cut them out and with them write out a sentence or thought. Doodle around them. (Label makers are fun to use, too!)

TOOLS TO USE!

LABEL MAKER

ABCDEFGHIJKLMNOP LABELS

SCISSORS

MOD PODGE

+

GLUE
GLUE {OR}

BRUSH

On My MUSIC PLAYER:

(Draw your music player — MP3,
iPod, etc. List, doodle, or collage
what songs are on it.)

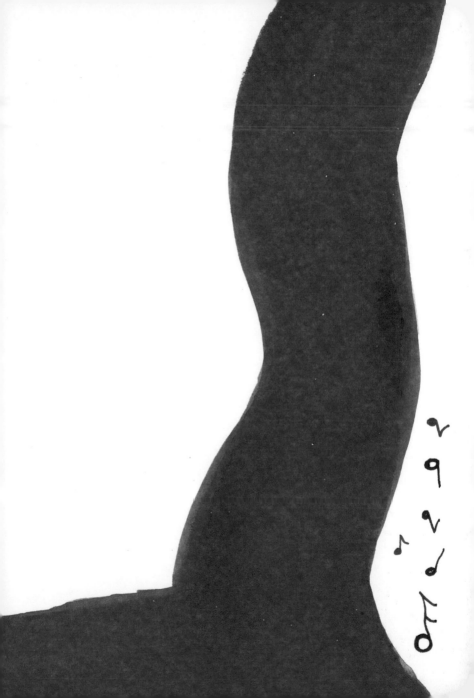

DOOdLed

NAME

NAME

RW

How to:

Cut out various types of letters that spell your name. Cut them out completely, so that there is |no| color behind them. Paste them down here to spell your name. Doodle inside each one.

GO GReEn

Use junk mail, a ticket stub, a wrapper, excess wrapping paper, a paper cup — anything! Don't throw it away — art it up! Doodle around it . . . Fill the whole page with recycled items. Maybe it's just a big collage of stuff with doodles!

i think

the perfect day would be . . .

I am Looking Forward to:

1)
2)
3)
4)
5)

MY moods

➡️ Mood rings were all the rage
in the '70s. They changed color as
the wearer's mood changed . . .
Get ready to make a mood page!

➡️ *fill* the shapes with colors
you feel express your moods.
Also doodle to define the moods.

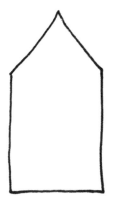

My friends

Find photos of your friends. Cut them out and paste them down into the frames on these pages. Doodle and write about each of them. Why do you hang out with them?

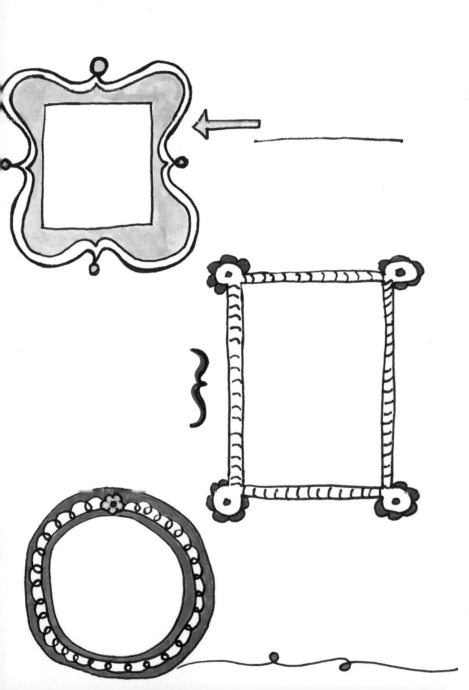

Find a recent picture of you and make a photocopy. Cut it out and paste it down on the page. How are you feeling TODAY? You can experience many emotions in a day. Happy, sad, tired, frustrated, ecstatic, angry, silly. Also, what are your plans for the day? Make it great!

SPILL it

TIME to let loose
and do whatever you
want on these pages. Doodle,
collage, write, color — it's up to you!
Create pages based on your day or
something fun you did!

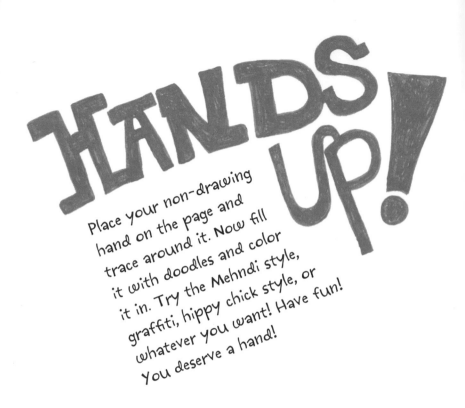

HANDS UP!

Place your non-drawing hand on the page and trace around it. Now fill it in with doodles and color it in. Try the Mehndi style, graffiti, hippy chick style, or whatever you want! Have fun! You deserve a hand!

DOODLE PLAY

What's your favorite game to play? Draw a picture, doodle, collage, or write it . . . Monopoly, Uno, chess, Candyland, Scrabble, Taboo?

word
Play

Find the letters
of your **FAVORITE** word
in magazines and cut them out.

LIKE THIS: GO

Paste them down on
the page any way that looks
cool. The letters can even fill
the page, like a collage. Doodle
around them; use various
colors and bits of collage.

HAVE fun!

INSTANT

~ memories ~

1} Find a photo of a relative —
   make sure to use a photocopy.

2: Paste the photo somewhere on the page.

3= Write and doodle about this relative —
   what you remember about them, how
   they've influenced you, what part they've
   played in your life, if any.

tool Tip: **TRY** adhering your photos
by using Scotch tape over the
edges or use photo corners.
It's artsy to show how the
image is attached to the page.

a week in my life

Doodle, write, or add paper or flat items from each day. Make sure to include the date and what you did that day.

Sunday

Monday

Tuesday

Wednesday

Thursday

Friday

Saturday

DOODLED {ALPHABET}

DRAW an outline of a letter and then doodle inside of it some words and things you associate with it. Maybe you drew an "S". Write down all the words you can think of starting with an "S".

✸ Use this list as inspiration for the doodles inside of the letter you've drawn.

MY List:

CARtoon fun

* Use a comic strip or an image of your favorite cartoon character. Imagine becoming that character. What would you do?

What's HOT

TiME to be a style watchdog!
What's hot and what's not? Find images.

What's NOT!

Cut and paste, doodle and write.
Include colors, patterns, and words.

Cool Summer

What I did on my summer vacation or what I plan to do . . .

I SPY

Look around. What do you see? List it out, then doodle it!

TOOL TIP:
Got a camera? Take photos of what you see and paste them down.

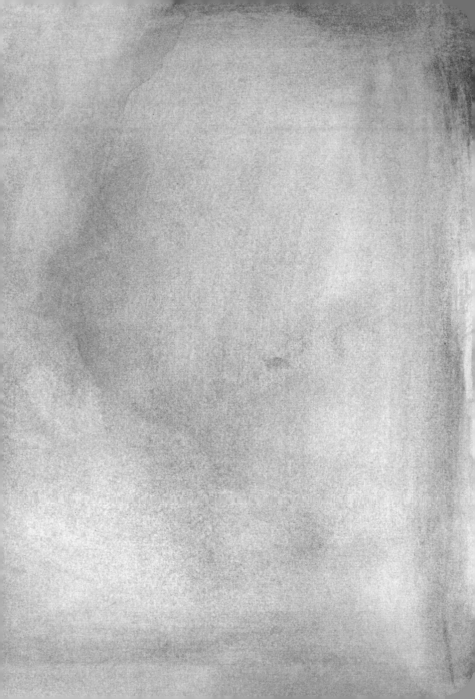

tool tip: ~ ø

Try to use different
kinds of pens, markers,
and pencils here. It
    will add variety!

MY LANDSCAPE

City, country,
mountains, desert?
Doodle and collage
your fave landscape.

doodle ME

Who would you like to be and why? Put yourself in that person's shoes and create a page that that person might have designed using your doodling and collage expertise.

WHAT I Like aBout me

Find a photo of you and cut yourself out of it. Paste it down — take a good look. How cool is that girl? Imagine you're her friend and write and doodle everything you like about her.

Even if you don't have an iPod or MP3 player, you can still bling one up! How would YOU decorate it?

TIP: Use glitter glue and/or paste down sequins and buttons, to bling it up!

MAKE ME Over

Find a photo of just
your face and paste
it down, then doodle
and collage over it
how you want your
hair and makeup.

About the Author

Dawn DeVries Sokol is the author of 1000 ARTIST JOURNAL PAGES (Quarry, 2008), a book designer, and an avid art journaler and doodler. For Sokol, getting started art journaling was the most difficult part, so she featured journal prompts (Art Journal Fridays) on her blog, www.dblogala.com, to help others get started journaling. She now teaches online workshops through her blog, and her art journal pages have been published on blogs and in books and exhibited in gallery shows from Tempe, Arizona, to Tokyo, Japan. She lives in Tempe, Arizona, with her husband, TJ, and their dog, Lucy.